TRUST 1 LORD

Skipping Gray Monitors

Published by Skipping Gray Monitors, 2024.

While every precaution has been taken in the preparation of this book, the publisher assumes no responsibility for errors or omissions, or for damages resulting from the use of the information contained herein.

TRUST 1 LORD

First edition. September 1, 2024.

Copyright © 2024 Skipping Gray Monitors.

ISBN: 979-8991232906

Written by Skipping Gray Monitors.

Table of Contents

Introduction 1
Beginning 3
Abraham 10
Isaac and Jacob 16
Lords People 27
The Ark 33
Judah 36
Flood 55
Lords' words 58
Clearings 67

Introduction

This is lord talking to you from heaven above, the words in this book are coming from me. The author channeled with me the 1611 King James Bible to create this story. This book was written for the author to understand what lord is trying to say to the author about life here. To understand in lords' words how we were created on this planet. Now that the author is familiar with lords' way of living. The author now can learn another way of living life that is more directed towards what the author's lord wants.

The author had negative thoughts and had constant suffering internally. Upon getting advice, the author found a person that cleared Akashic records. This concept was new to the author. After the clearing was done the author felt better and took a course on Akashic record clearing. To understand what is currently on a souls Akashic record, the use of a pointed stone hanging from a chain was needed for the class. At first the stone would not move, but with persistence and time it would move. Understand, trust yourself.

The author performed free readings but received disrespect from most of these people, it was discouraging. So, instead of helping others, the author used this information to help self-heal on a regular basis. When the mind would race with negative thoughts the author was advised to write these thoughts down. At this point the author was taught to clear each one of these wounds one at a time, and this eliminated negative thoughts. The information and guidance came from using the pointed stone attached to a chain.

After some time, the author started talking to lord. When this happened, lord started to listen and responded by telling the author to use the hands instead of the pointed stone and chain for guidance. Then was taught to spell out words with both hands and then with each word using only the first letter of each word was necessary to confirm the voice of lord in the head. It took a year to learn this entire process.

SKIPPING GRAY MONITORS

After this the author was guided to read the bible, not wanting too though. Lord made the author read this book three times, to learn the hand guidance, before he started guiding this short story, called channeling. Each scripture was chosen specifically by lord then it was arranged according to timeline. The guidance from lord was always, trust lord.

Isaiah 45:25 In lord shall all the seed of Israel be justified, and shall glory.

Isaiah 49:1 Listen, O, unto me, and hearken ye people from far. The Lord hath called me, my name.

Isaiah 49:2 And he hath made my mouth like a sharp sword, in the shadow of his hand hath he hid me, and made me a polished shaft;

Isaiah 49:3 And said to me; Thou art my servant, O, in whom I will be glorified.

Isaiah 49:4 Then I said, I have labored in vain, I have spent my strength for naught, and in vain: yet surely my judgment is with lord, and my work with my lord.

Isaiah 49:6 And he said, it is a light thing that thou shouldest be my servant to raise up the tribes of Jacob, and to restore the preserved of Israel: that thou mayest be my salvation, to earth.

Isaiah 50:4 Lord, he wakeneth morning by morning, he wakeneth mine ear to hear, learn.

Isaiah 50:5 Lord hath opened mine ear, I was not rebellious.

Sirach 51:12 For thou saved me from destruction, and delivered me from the evil time: therefore, will I give thanks and praise thee, and bless thy name, o lord.

Judges 14:18 What is sweeter than honey? And what is stronger than a Lion? If ye had not plowed, my heifer, ye not found out riddle.

Beginning

Genesis 1:1 In the beginning lord created the earth.

Genesis 1:16 He made the stars also.

II Esdras 6:45 Thou commanded that the sun should shine, and the moon give light,

II Esdras 6:46 and gave them a charge to do service unto.

Zechariah 14:9 Lord be king over all the earth: there be one lord, and his name 1.

Psalms 93:1 The lord reigneth, with strength: the world also is established, that it cannot be moved.

Psalms 93:2 Thy throne is established of old: thou art from everlasting.

Psalms 96:10 Lord reigneth: the world also that be established that it shall not be moved.

Isaiah 41:4 I lord, the first, and with the last; I am he.

Deuteronomy 32:40 For I lift up my hand to heaven, and say, I live forever.

Genesis 2:4 These are the generations of the earth when they were created.

I John 1:1 That which from the beginning, which we have seen with our eyes, which we have looked upon, of the world.

I John 1:2 Life was manifested.

Genesis 2:7 Lord formed man of the dust of the ground, and breathed into his nostrils the breath of life and man became a living soul.

St. John 5:26 For as the father hath life in himself: so hath he given to the to have life in self.

Job 9:9 Which maketh us Pleiades.

Deuteronomy 14:21 Thou an alien: for thou art a holy people unto lord.

I Corinthians 15:39 All flesh is the same flesh, there is one kind of flesh.

SKIPPING GRAY MONITORS

Genesis 1:27 So lord created man in his own image, in the image of lord created he. Male female created he them.

St. Matthew 19:4 At the beginning, made them male female.

Genesis 1:21 Lord created great whales, and every living creature that move, which the waters brought forth abundantly, lord saw that it was good.

Lords' words: Centuries went by.

Genesis 1:9 And lord said, let the waters under the heaven be gathered together unto one place, and let the dry land appear: and it was so.

Genesis 1:11 Lord said, let the earth bring forth grass, the herb yielding seed, and the fruit tree yielding fruit after his kind, whose seed is in itself, upon the earth: and it was so.

Ezekiel 29:9 Know that I am Lord: The river is mine, and I have made it.

Lords' words: Centuries went by. We were monster snakes then, in many forms.

II Esdras 6:53 Upon the day thou gave command to the earth, that before thee it should bring forth creeping things.

Genesis 1:24 The earth bring forth the living creature, his kind, creeping thing, beast of the earth, and it was so.

Lords' words: Centuries went by. The snakes evolved; some could fly to escape being picked on by larger snakes. Teeth became a protection for some to stunt so they could escape and hide, teeth became a way to eat more food for others, four claw feet came out on some to travel. This is our family.

Genesis 1:20 And lord said, let the waters bring forth abundantly the moving creature that hath life, and fowl that may fly above the earth.

Genesis 1:22 And lord blessed them.

Lords' words: Hooved monsters were next to be evolved.

TRUST 1 LORD

Genesis 1:25 The beast of the earth after his kind, cattle after their kind, and everything that creepeth upon the earth after his kind: and lord saw that it was good.

Genesis 1:29 Lord said, behold, I have given you every herb bearing seed, which is upon the face of all the earth, and every tree, in the which is the fruit of a tree yielding seed, to you it shall be for meat.

Genesis 1:30 To every beast of the earth. To everything that creepeth upon the earth, wherein there is life, I have given every green herb for meat: and it was so.

Genesis 2:9 And out of the ground, lord grow every tree that is pleasant to the sight, and good for food; the tree of life in the midst of the garden.

Genesis 2:16 Of every tree of thou mayest freely eat.

Sirach 30:15 Health and good state of body, a strong body.

Lords' words: Gray Monitor was the first snake to listen to lords' voice. It is white upon the belly, it has claws and feet like our own and some stood up on their back feet.

Genesis 3:1 Now the serpent was more subtle than any beast of the field.

Ezekiel 19:10 Thy mother is in thy blood, planted, she was fruitful and full of reason.

I Samuel 14:13 And climbed up upon hands and upon feet.

I Samuel 17:37 The paw of the Lyon, and the paw of the Bear, me of the hand of this Philistine.

I Samuel 19:2 Thyself abide in a secret place, and hide myself.

II Samuel 1:25 Thou wast in thine high places.

II Samuel 14:25 From the sole of his foot even to the crown of his head, there was no blemish in him.

Isaiah 13:22 The wild beasts of the islands in their desolate houses, dragons in their pleasant palaces.

Exodus 14:3 They are entangled in the land, the wilderness.

I Esdras 8:91 Lying flat upon the ground, among the multitude.

SKIPPING GRAY MONITORS

Exodus 26:3 Coupled together one to another: and other shall be coupled one to another.

Exodus 26:9 And thou shalt couple by themselves.

Exodus 26:10 And thou shalt make loops on the edge of the one that is outmost in the coupling, of the which coupleth the second.

Exodus 26:5 The loops take hold one of another.

Exodus 26:11 And thou shalt make into the loops, and couple the together, that it may be one.

Exodus 26:6 And it shall be one.

Exodus 26:7 And thou shalt make to be upon the, eleven shalt thou make.

Deuteronomy 22:6 The eggs, thou shalt not take the.

Exodus 26:8 The length of one shall be thirty, and the breadth of one four, the eleven shall be all of one measure.

Lords' words: They snuggled, like human feet and legs do.

Genesis 3:8 They heard the voice of lord, walking in the garden in the cool of the day: and hid themselves from the presence of lord amongst the trees of the garden.

Exodus 20:18 And all saw the thundering, and the lightning, and the noise, and the mountain smoking: when the saw it, they removed, and stood afar off.

Exodus 20:19 Lest we die.

Numbers 26:10 The fire devoured, and became a sign.

Genesis 6:1 When men began to multiply.

Genesis 6:4 They were giants in the earth in those days: when the sons came in to the daughters, they bare children.

II Samuel 1:20 The daughters of the Philistines rejoice, the daughters of the uncircumcised.

II Samuel 21:18 The Philistines, which was of the sons of the giants.

I Chronicles 20:4 The Philistines; at which time, the children of the giant.

TRUST 1 LORD

I Samuel 14:19 The Philistines went on and increased: with thine hand.

Exodus 10:15 For they covered the face of the whole earth, so that the land was darkened; and they did eat every herb of the land, and all the fruit of the trees.

Lords' words: Centuries went by. Food became scarce and monsters with teeth began to eat each other if they were slow and hid not.

II Esdras 4:4 I shall shew thee from whence the wicked heart cometh.

Deuteronomy 5:17 Thou shalt not kill.

Numbers 11:17 The spirit which is upon thee, thou bear it thyself alone.

Leviticus 11:26 Of every beast which divideth the hoof, and is not cloven footed, nor cheweth the cud, are unclean to you.

Leviticus 11:3 Parteth the hoof, and is cloven footed, & cheweth cud among the beasts.

Deuteronomy 14:6 And every beast that parteth the hoof, and cleaveth the cleft into two claws, and cheweth the cud amongst the beasts.

Deuteronomy 14:7 Nevertheless ye shall not eat, of them that chew the cud, or of them that divide the cloven hoof; as the camel, and the hare, and the coney: for they chew the cud, but divide not the hoof.

Leviticus 11:4 Them that divide the hoof: as the camel, he cheweth the cud, but divideth not the hoof, he is unclean to you.

Leviticus 11:5 The conie, he cheweth the cud, but divideth not the hoof, he is unclean to you.

Leviticus 11:6 And the hare, he cheweth the cud, but divideth not the hoof, he is unclean to you.

Leviticus 11:7 And the swine, though he divide the hoof, and be cloven footed, yet he cheweth not the cud; he is unclean to you.

SKIPPING GRAY MONITORS

Deuteronomy 14:8 And the swine, it divideth the hoof, yet cheweth not the cud, it is unclean to you: ye shall not eat of their flesh, nor touch their dead carcass.

Leviticus 11:8 Of their flesh shall ye not eat, and their carcass shall ye not touch; they are unclean to you.

Leviticus 11:9 Whatsoever hath fins and scales in the waters, in the seas, and in the rivers,

Leviticus 11:10 and all that have not fins nor scales in the seas, and in the rivers, of all that move in the waters, and of any living thing which is in the waters, they shall be an abomination unto you.

Leviticus 11:13 Among the fowls; they are an eagle, and the ossifrage, and the osprey,

Leviticus 11:14 and the vulture, and the kite after his kind;

Leviticus 11:16 and the owl, and the night hawk, and the cuckoo, and the hawk after his kind,

Leviticus 11:17 and the little owl, and the cormorant, and the great owl,

Leviticus 11:18 and the swan, and the pelican, and the gier eagle,

Leviticus 11:19 and the stork, the heron after her kind, and the lapwing, and the bat.

Leviticus 11:20 All fowls that creep, going upon all four, that be an abomination unto you.

Leviticus 11:21 Every flying creeping thing that goeth upon all four, which have legs above their feet, to leap withal upon the earth;

Leviticus 11:22 the locust after his kind, and the bald locust after his kind, and the beetle after his kind, and the grasshopper after his kind.

Leviticus 11:23 All other flying creeping things, which have four feet, they all be an abomination unto you.

Leviticus 11:27 And whatsoever goeth upon his paws, among all manner of beasts that go on all four, those are unclean to you.

Leviticus 11:29 Among the creeping things that creep upon the earth; the weasel, and the mouse, and the tortoise after his kind,

TRUST 1 LORD

Leviticus 11:30 and the ferret, and the chameleon, and the lizard, and the snail, and the mole.

Leviticus 11:42 Whatsoever goeth upon the belly, and whatsoever goeth upon all four, or whatsoever hath more feet among all creeping things that creep upon the earth, them ye shall not eat, for they are an abomination.

Lords' words: Centuries went by.

Abraham

Joshua 24:2 Terah, the father of Abraham:

I Samuel 14:33 the sin against lord, in that they eat with the blood. Ye have transgressed.

Numbers 30:6 Wherewith bound soul.

Hebrews 5:14 Meat belongeth to them that are of full rage, those who by reason of use have their senses exercised to discern both good and evil.

Exodus 23:21 Beware of him, provoke him not; for he will not pardon your transgressions.

Leviticus 20:4 The of the land do any ways hide their eyes from the man, his seed kill him.

Exodus 23:11 Rest and lie still; they leave the beasts of the field. In like manner thou shalt deal with thy.

Leviticus 20:5 Then I will set my face against that man, and against his family, and will cut him off, from among their people.

Leviticus 20:6 And the soul that turneth after such as have familiar spirits, to go after them, I will even set my face against that soul, and will cut him off from among his people.

Leviticus 20:7 Sanctify yourselves therefore, and be ye holy: for I am the Lord your god.

II Esdras 3:13 Now when they lived so wickedly before thee, thou didst choose thee a man from among them, whose name was Abraham.

Genesis 21:34 And Abraham sojourned in the Philistines' land, many days.

I Samuel 9:2 From his shoulders and upward he was higher than any of the people.

II Samuel 13:3 The was a very subtle man.

I Samuel 16:7 Lord seeth not as man seeth; for man looketh on the outward appearance, but lord looketh on the heart.

TRUST 1 LORD

II Esdras 16:54 Behold, lord knoweth all the works of men, their imaginations, their thoughts, and their hearts.

Exodus 21:29 The ox were to push with his horn, he hath killed, the ox shall be stoned, be put to death.

Deuteronomy 4:36 He made thee to hear his voice, that he might instruct thee.

I Samuel 22:23 Abide thou with me, fear not: for he that seeketh life seeketh thy life: with me thou shalt be in safeguard.

Exodus 15:26 If thou wilt diligently hearken to the voice of lord, and will do that which is right in his sight, and wilt give ear to this command. I am the lord that healeth thee.

Deuteronomy 5:33 You shall walk in all the ways which lord hath commanded you, that ye may live, and that it may be well with you, and that ye may prolong your days in the land which ye shall possess.

Deuteronomy 7:6 For thou art an holy people to lord: lord hath chosen thee to be a special people unto himself, above all people that are upon the face of the earth.

Deuteronomy 7:9 Know therefore that lord, he is faithful, which keepeth mercy with them that love him, to a thousand generations.

Deuteronomy 11:26 Behold, I set before you this day, a blessing and a curse:

Deuteronomy 11:27 a blessing, if ye obey lord, which I command you this day:

Deuteronomy 11:28 and a curse, if ye will not obey.

Genesis 3:5 For lord doeth know that in the day your eyes shall be opened: and ye shall be as lords, knowing good and evil.

Deuteronomy 31:7 Be strong and of a good courage: for thou must go to land which the lord hath it.

Deuteronomy 31:8 And lord, he it is that doth go before thee, he will be with thee, he will not fail thee, neither forsake thee: fear not, neither be dismayed.

SKIPPING GRAY MONITORS

Numbers 15:16 One law, and one manner shall be for you, and for the stranger that sojourneth with you.

Numbers 15:18 When ye come into the land whither I bring you,

Numbers 15:22 if ye have erred, and not observed all these commands which lord hath spoken,

Numbers 15:24 then it shall be by ignorance without the knowledge of the, young bullock.

Numbers 16:5 Lord will shew who are his, and who is holy.

Exodus 4:31 Bow the head and worship.

I Samuel 16:23 And the evil spirit upon departed from him.

I Samuel 19:6 Lord liveth, he shall not be slain.

Genesis 20:1 Abraham journeyed.

Judges 9:1 And Abimelech went to.

Judges 9:19 Rejoice ye in Abimelech, and let him also rejoice in you.

Judges 14:20 His companion, whom he had used as his friend.

Genesis 17:22 And he left off talking with him, and lord went.

Numbers 14:24 He had another spirit with him, (and hath followed fully) him will I bring to the land where into he went; and his seed shall possess it.

Deuteronomy 11:12 A land, which lord careth for: the eyes of lord are always upon it, from the beginning of the year even unto the end of the year.

Exodus 15:27 And they came to where were water, and trees, and they encamped there by the waters.

Numbers 33:37 And they pitched in mount Hor, in the edge of the land of Edom.

Numbers 33:38 Mount Hor, the land of Egypt.

Numbers 21:4 And they journeyed from mount Hor, by the way of the red sea, to compass the land of Edom: and the foul of the people was much discouraged because of the way.

Deuteronomy 1:29 Then I said to you, dread not, neither be afraid of them.

TRUST 1 LORD

Deuteronomy 20:3 To battle: let not your hearts faint, fear not, and do not tremble, neither be ye terrified because of them.

Numbers 21:6 Serpents among the, they bit the and much died.

Deuteronomy 1:30 The lord which goeth before you, he shall fight for you, according to all that he did for you in Egypt before your eyes.

Deuteronomy 20:4 For lord is he that goeth with you, to fight for you against your enemies.

Deuteronomy 26:18 Lord hath thee to be his peculiar people, and that thou shouldest keep all his commands:

Deuteronomy 26:19 and to make thee high above all nations which he hath made, in praise, and in name, and in honor, and that thou mayest be an holy people to lord.

Genesis 11:2 And it came to pass, as they journeyed, that they found a plain in the land and they dwelt there.

Deuteronomy 30:1 Lord thy hath driven thee,

Deuteronomy 30:2 thy shalt obey his voice according to all, this day, thou and thy children, with all thine heart, and with all thy soul.

II Esdras 6:44 For immediately there was great and innumerable fruit, and many divers' pleasures for the taste, & flowers of unchangeable color, and odors of wonderful smell.

Leviticus 26:4 I will give you rain in due season, and the land shall yield her increase, and the trees of the field shall yield their fruit.

Numbers 22:4 The ox licketh up the grass of the field at that time.

Genesis 13:10 All the plain, it was well watered everywhere before lord, even as the garden of lord, the land of Egypt.

Genesis 14:19 And he blessed the most high lord, possessor of heaven and earth.

Exodus 18:3 I have been an alien in a strange land.

Exodus 18:14 The sittest thyself alone, and all stand by thee from morning to even.

I Samuel 3:1 In those days; there was no vision.

SKIPPING GRAY MONITORS

Deuteronomy 29:6 Ye have not eaten bread, neither have you drunk wine or strong drink: ye know that I am lord.

Joshua 24:7 Ye dwelt in the wilderness a long season.

Genesis 15:2 Abram said, seeing I go childless.

Genesis 22:13 Abraham lifted up his eyes, and looked, and behold behind him a ram caught in a thicket by horns: and Abraham went and took the ram.

II Samuel 17:19 The thing was not known.

Deuteronomy 29:3 The great temptations which thine eyes have seen, those great miracles.

Numbers 17:5 And it shall come to pass, that the man whom I shall choose, shall blossom.

Galatians 4:22 For it is written, that Abraham had two sons, the one by a bondmaid, the other by a free-woman.

Genesis 3:14 And lord said to the serpent, because thou has done this, thou art above all cattle, and above every beast of the field, all the days of thy life.

Genesis 1:28 And lord blessed them, and lord said to them, be fruitful, and multiply, and the earth, subdue it.

Genesis 28:11 And he lighted up a certain place, and tarried there all night.

Exodus 29:1 Take one young bullock, two rams without blemish.

Exodus 29:35 Seven days shalt thou consecrate them.

Exodus 27:2 His horns shall be of the same.

Exodus 29:12 Bullock, and put it upon the horns of the.

Genesis 31:10 The rams which leaped upon the cattle were ringstraked, speckled, and grisled.

Exodus 29:42 This shall be a continual throughout generations. Where will meet you, to speak there unto thee.

Romans 4:3 Abraham believed lord, and it was to him righteousness.

Sirach 44:19 Abraham was a great father of many people: in glory.

TRUST 1 LORD

Sirach 44:20 Who kept the law of the most high, he established in his flesh; he was faithful.

I John 4:12 No man has seen lord at any time. If we love one another, lord dwelleth in us, and his love is perfected in us.

Romans 4:16 Therefore all the seed of Abraham, who is the father of us all,

Romans 5:19 for as by one man's disobedience many were made sinners: so by the obedience of one, shall many be made righteous.

Genesis 15:9 He said to him, take me a heifer of three years old, and a she goat of three years old.

Genesis 15:10 And he took unto him all these.

Genesis 18:7 Abraham ran unto the herd, and fetched a calf, tender and good, and gave it unto a young man; and he hasted to it.

II Esdras 5:26 And of all the fowls that are created, thou has named thee one dove: and of all the cattle that are made, thou hast provided thee one sheep.

II Esdras 5:27 And among all the multitudes of peoples, thou hast gotten thee one people: and unto this people whom thou lovedst, thou gavest a law that is approved of all.

II Esdras 8:4 So answered I and said, my foul, understand and devour wisdom.

I Samuel 23:27 For the Philistines have invaded the land.

Genesis 20:14 And Abimelech took sheep and oxen, and men-servants, and women servants, and gave them unto Abraham.

Genesis 21:27 And Abraham took sheep and oxen, and gave them to Abimelech; and both of them made a covenant.

Joshua 10:11 They were more which died with hailstorms, then they whom the children slew.

Genesis 21:32 Then Abimelech rose up, and they returned into the land of the Philistines.

Isaac and Jacob

Genesis 1:26 Lord said, let us make man in our image, after our likeness.

Ruth 4:7 Now this the time for confirm all things; man, this was.

Genesis 25:21 Isaac entreated lord, for his was barren: and lord entreated of him, and Rebekah, conceived.

Genesis 26:14 For he had possession of flocks, and servants, and the Philistines envied him.

Genesis 26:15 For all the wells which his father's servants had digged in the days of Abraham, his father, the Philistines had stopped them, and filled them with earth.

Genesis 26:18 Isaac digged again the wells of water, which they had digged in the days of Abraham his father: for the Philistines had stopped them after the death of Abraham, and he called their names after the names by which his father had called them.

Genesis 25:22 And the children struggled together within her.

II Esdras 8:8 For the body is fashioned in the mother's womb, and thou give it members, thy creature, and nine months does thy workmanship endure thy creature which is created in her.

II Esdras 8:10 Out of the breasts milk to be given, which is the fruit of the breasts.

II Esdras 8:11 That the thing which is fashioned, may be nourished for a time.

Genesis 25:24 There were twins in her womb.

Genesis 25:25 The first came out red, all over like a hairy garment: and they called his name Esau.

Genesis 25:26 And after that came his brother out, and his hand took hold on Esau's heel; and his name was called Jacob.

II Esdras 6:8 And he said unto me, from Abraham unto Isaac, when Jacob and Esau were born of him, Jacob's hand held first the heel of Esau.

Judges 18:10 Unto a people lord hath given your hands.

TRUST 1 LORD

II Esdras 6:9 Of the world, Jacob is the beginning of it that followeth.

II Esdras 6:10 The hand of man is.

Leviticus 26:13 I have made you go upright.

Job 1:1 Man was perfect and upright and eschewed evil.

Revelation 9:19 For their tails were like unto serpents, and had heads, and with them they do hurt.

Genesis 17:17 Then Abraham fell upon his face, and laughed, and said in his heart, shall a child be born unto him that is a bear?

Genesis 21:6 And Sarah said, Lord hath made me to laugh, so that all that hear, will laugh with me.

Genesis 27:11 Jacob said to Rebekah his mother, behold, Esau my brother is a hairy man, and I am a smooth man.

I Samuel 2:19 Moreover his mother made a little coat, and brought it to him from year to year, yearly.

Genesis 3:21 Unto, did lord make coats of skins and clothed them.

Leviticus 13:48 Anything made of skin.

Leviticus 13:49 The be greenish or reddish in the garment, or in the skin, or in any thing of skin.

Genesis 27:27 And he smelled the smell of his raiment. The smell of my son is as the smell of a field, which lord hath blessed.

Deuteronomy 33:10 They shall teach Jacob judgments, and Israel thy law.

Tobit 4:17 Give nothing to the wicked.

Tobit 4:19 Bless lord always, and desire of him that thy ways may be directed, and that all thy paths, and counsels may prosper: lord himself giveth.

Tobit 4:21 Depart from sin, and do that which is pleasing in his sight.

Wisdom of Solomon 9:16 Hardly do we guess aright at the things that are upon the earth, and the things that are before us: who hath searched out?

SKIPPING GRAY MONITORS

Wisdom of Solomon 9:17 And thy counsel who hath known, except thou give wisdom, thy holy spirit from above.

Wisdom of Solomon 9:18 For the ways of them which lived on the earth were saved through wisdom.

Sirach 1:1 All wisdom cometh from lord, and is with him forever.

Genesis 27:41 And Esau hated Jacob because of the blessing, wherewith his father blessed him: and Esau, in his heart, the days of mourning for my father are at hand, then will I slay my brother Jacob.

Deuteronomy 1:17 Ye shall be afraid of the face of man.

Lords' words: Jacob went away to find a different female.

Esther 16:10 Being indeed a stranger, and far different from our goodness, received of us.

Esther 16:11 Had so far forth obtained the favor that we shew toward every nation, as that he was called our father, and was continually honored of all men.

Tobit 4:12 Abraham, Isaac, and Jacob: remember, that our fathers from the beginning, even that they all, wives of their own kindred, and were blessed in their children, and their seed shall inherit the land.

Tobit 4:13 Love thy brethren, the sons and daughters of thy people,

Hebrews 11:21 Jacob, leaning upon the top of his staff.

Esther 13:2 I purposed to settle my subjects continually in a quiet life, and making my kingdom peaceable, to renew peace which is desired of all men.

Genesis 9:8 And lord spake to, saying,

Genesis 9:9 I establish my covenant with you, and with your seed after you.

Exodus 6:7 I will take you to me for a people, and I will be to you a lord: and ye shall know that I am the lord.

Numbers 2:2 Children of Israel shall pitch by his own standard.

Exodus 29:45 And I will dwell among the children of Israel, and will be their lord.

TRUST 1 LORD

Exodus 29:46 And they shall know that I am lord their lord, that I dwell among them.

Isaiah 27:6 He shall cause them that come of Jacob to take root: blossom and bud, and fill the face of the world with fruit.

Isaiah 28:4 And the glorious beauty which is on the head of the fat, shall be a fading flower, and as the fruit: which when he that looketh upon it, seeth it, while it is yet in his hand he eateth it up.

Isaiah 28:5 In that day shall lord be for a crown of glory, and for a diadem of beauty unto the residue of his people.

Isaiah 28:6 And for judgment to him that sitteth in judgment, and for strength to them that turn the to the.

Isaiah 28:15 For we have made lies our refuge, and under falsehood have we hid ourselves.

Isaiah 28:16 Therefore thus saith lord, I lay a foundation, a sure foundation: he that believe, shall not make haste.

Genesis 32:12 And thou said, I will surely do thee good, and make thy seed as the sand of the sea, which cannot be numbered for multitude.

Isaiah 28:25 When he hath made plain thereof, the principal

Isaiah 28:26 to discretion.

Isaiah 28:29 This also cometh forth from lord, which is wonderful in counsel, and excellent in working.

Exodus 28:3 And thou shalt speak to all that are wise-hearted, whom I have filled with the spirit of wisdom.

Numbers 18:15 Everything that openeth the matrix in all flesh, shall be thine: the firstborn of man shalt thou surely redeem.

Exodus 34:19 All that openeth the matrix is mine: and every firstling amongst thy cattle, whether ox or sheep.

II Esdras 5:7 Which many have not known: but they shall all hear the voice thereof.

Isaiah 29:4 Thy voice shall be as of one that hath a familiar spirit, and thy speech shall whisper.

Isaiah 29:5 Yea, it shall be at an instant suddenly.

SKIPPING GRAY MONITORS

Isaiah 29:13 Lips do honor me, but have removed their heart far from me, and their fear towards me is taught by the precept of men.

Isaiah 29:14 Therefore behold, I will proceed to do a marvelous work amongst this people, even a marvelous work and a wonder: for the wisdom of the and the understanding of the prudent shall be hid.

Isaiah 30:30 And lord shall cause his glorious voice to be heard, and shall shew the lighting of arm.

Isaiah 32:15 The spirit be poured upon us from high, the wilderness be a fruitful field, and the fruitful field be counted for a forest.

Isaiah 32:16 Then shall dwell in wilderness, and righteousness remain in the fruitful field.

Isaiah 32:17 And the work of righteousness shall be peace, and the effect of righteousness, quietness.

Isaiah 32:18 And my people shall dwell in a peaceable habitation, and in sure dwellings, and in quiet resting places.

Isaiah 37:30 Ye shall eat this year such as groweth of itself: and the second year that which springeth of the same: and in the third year sow ye and reap, and eat the fruit thereof.

Isaiah 39:6 Behold, the days come, that all that is in thine house, and that which thy fathers have laid up in store, until this day, shall be carried to: nothing shall be left, saith lord.

Isaiah 39:8 He said moreover, for there shall be peace and truth in my days.

Isaiah 41:6 They helped everyone his neighbor, and every one said to his brother, Be of good courage.

Sirach 28:7 Bear no malice to thy neighbor: remember the highest, and wink.

Genesis 11:1 The whole earth was of one language, and of one speech.

II Esdras 6:39 Silence were on every side; the sound of man's voice was not yet formed.

TRUST 1 LORD

Isaiah 46:3 House of Jacob, and all the remnant of the house of Israel, which are borne from the belly, which are carried from the womb.

Ezekiel 16:4 As for thy nativity in the day thou wast born, thy navel was not cut.

Genesis 49:1 And Jacob called unto his sons, and said, gather yourselves together, that I may tell you that which shall befall you.

Genesis 49:3 Reuben, thou art my firstborn, my might, the beginning of my strength, the excellency of dignity, and the excellency of power:

Genesis 49:4 unstable as water, thou shalt not excel; because thou went up to thy fathers bed: then defildest thou it: he went up to my couche.

Sirach 28:10 As a man's strength is, so is his wrath.

Sirach 8:16 Strive not with an angry man, for blood is as nothing in his sight, and where there is no help, he will overthrow thee.

Proverbs 6:32 who so committeth adultery lacketh understanding: he that doeth it, destroyeth his own soul.

Proverbs 6:33 A wound and dishonor shall he get, and his reproach shall not be wiped away.

Proverbs 6:34 For jealousy is the rage of man: therefore, he will not spare in the day of vengeance.

Proverbs 6:35 He will not regard any ransom; neither will he rest content, though thou givest many gifts.

Deuteronomy 33:6 Let Reuben live, not die.

Numbers 2:16 The camp of Reuben were set forth in the second rank.

Genesis 49:5 Simeon and Levi are brethren; instruments of cruelty are in their habitations.

Genesis 49:6 O my fowl, come not thou into their secret: unto their assembly mine honor be not thou united: for in their anger they slew man.

SKIPPING GRAY MONITORS

Genesis 49:7 Cursed be their anger, for it was fierce; and their wrath, for it was cruel: I will divide them in Jacob, and scatter them in Israel.

Leviticus 14:3 The plague of leprosy be in the leper.

Leviticus 22:4 Man soever of the seed of Aaron is a leper, or have a running issue.

Leviticus 22:8 That which dieth of itself, or is torn with beasts, he shall not eat to defile himself therewith.

Leviticus 22:9 They shall therefore keep mine ordinance, lest they bare sin for it.

Deuteronomy 33:8 Levi,

Deuteronomy 33:9 I have not seen him, neither did he acknowledge his brethren: nor knew his own children.

Genesis 38:7 And Judah's first born was wicked in the sight of lord, and lord slew him.

Genesis 38:12 Judah was comforted, and went up unto his sheep, his friend.

Genesis 49:8 Judah, thou art he whom thy brethren shall praise; thy hand shall be in the neck of thine enemies; thy father's children shall bow down before thee.

Genesis 49:9 Judah is a lion's whelp: from the prey my son, thou art gone up: he stooped down, he couched as a lion, and as an old lion: who shall rouse him up?

Genesis 49:10 The scepter shall not depart from Judah, and unto him shall the gathering of the people be:

Genesis 49:11 **binding his foal, his ass colt to the choice**. He washed his garments in wine, and his clothes in the blood of grapes.

Genesis 49:12 His eyes shall be red with wine, and his teeth white with milk.

Isaiah 28:1 Woe to the crown of pride, whose glorious beauty is a fading flower, which are on the head of them that overcome wine!

Job 11:12 For vain man, man be born a wild ass's colt.

Zechariah 9:9 The foal of an ass.

TRUST 1 LORD

Genesis 34:28 They took their sheep, and their asses, that was in the field.

Genesis 42:12 And he said unto them, nay.

Genesis 42:26 And they lade their asses with the come, and departed thence.

Deuteronomy 33:11 Bless, lord, his substance, accept the work of his hands, smite through the loins of them that rise against him, and of them that hate him, that they rise not again.

Genesis 49:13 Zebulun shall dwell at the haven of the sea; and he shall be for a haven of ships.

Deuteronomy 33:18 Zebulun in thy going out; and, Issachar, in thy tents.

Genesis 49:14 Issachar is a strong ass couching down between two burdens:

Genesis 49:15 and he saw that rest was good, and the land that it was pleasant; and bowed his shoulder to bare.

Genesis 49:17 Dan shall be a serpent by the way, an adder in the path, that biteth the horse heels, so that his rider shall fall backward.

Deuteronomy 33:22 Dan is a Lyon's whelp: he shall leap from.

Numbers 2:31 The camp of Dan shall go hindmost.

Genesis 49:19 Gad, a troop shall overcome him: but he shall overcome at the last.

Deuteronomy 33:20 Gad, blessed be he that enlargeth Gad: he dwelleth as a lion, and teareth the arm with the crown of the head.

Genesis 49:20 Out of Asher his bread shall be fat.

Judges 5:17 Asher, abode in his breaches.

Genesis 41:2 And behold, there came up out of the river seven well favored kine and fat fleshed; and they fed in a meadow.

Genesis 49:21 Naphtali is a hind let loose: he giveth goodly words.

Leviticus 16:22 And the goat shall bear upon him all their iniquities, unto a land not inhabited: and he shall let go the goat in the wilderness.

SKIPPING GRAY MONITORS

Judges 7:18 I blow a trumpet, I and all that are with me blow trumpet.

Deuteronomy 33:23 Naphtali satisfied with favor.

Genesis 37:2 Joseph being seventeen years old, was feeding the flock with his brethren. Joseph brought unto his father their evil report.

Genesis 3:22 Lord said, behold, the man is become as one of us, to know good and evil. Now lest he put forth his hand.

Genesis 37:3 Israel loved Joseph, and he made a coat of many colors.

Genesis 37:26 And Judah said unto his brethren, what profit is it if we slay our brother, and conceal his blood?

Deuteronomy 33:13 Joseph for the deep that coucheth beneath.

Genesis 49:22 Joseph is a fruitful bough, whose branches run over the wall.

Genesis 49:24 Abode in strength, the arms of his hands were made strong: **from thence is the shepherd**, the stone of Israel.

James 3:7 Of beasts, is tamed, and hath been tamed mankind.

Genesis 37:7 We were binding sheaves in the field.

Genesis 37:25 And they sat down to eat bread.

Numbers 2:24 The camp of Ephraim were in the third rank.

Lords' words: Jacob had four woman and eleven children when he decided to go back home.

I Esdras 8:50 And there I bowed unto our lord, to desire of him a prosperous journey, both for us, and them that were with us: for our children and for the cattle.

I Esdras 8:52 The power of lord, be with them that seek him, to support them in all ways.

I Esdras 8:53 We besought our lord, and found him favorable unto us.

I Esdras 8:70 For both they, and their sons have with their daughters, and the holy seed is mixed with the strange people of the land, and from the beginning of this matter, the rulers and the great men have been partakers of this iniquity.

Genesis 29:17 Leah was tender eyed.

Genesis 32:17 He commanded the, saying, when Esau my brother meeteth thee, and asketh thee, saying, whose are thou and whither goest thou and whose are these before thee?

Genesis 32:18 Then thou shalt say, they be thy servant, Jacobs.

Genesis 32:21 Himself lodged that night in the company.

Genesis 32:22 And he rose up that night, and took his two women, and his two women servants, and his eleven sons, and passed over the.

Genesis 33:3 He bowed himself to the ground.

Genesis 33:4 And Esau ran to meet him, and embraced him, and kissed him, and they wept.

Genesis 32:24 And Jacob there wrestled a man with him, until the breaking of the day.

Genesis 35:16 And they journeyed and Rachel travailed, and she had hard labour.

Genesis 35:17 it came to pass when she was in hard labour, that the said to her, Fear not; thou shalt have this son also.

Genesis 35:18 And it came to pass, she died.

Genesis 49:27 Benjamin shall ravin as a wolf: in the morning he shall devour the prey, and at night he shall divide the spoil.

Deuteronomy 33:12 Benjamin he shall dwell between his shoulders.

Genesis 43:34 And he took and sent messes unto them from before him: but Benjamin's mess was five times so much as any of theirs: and they drank, and were merry with him.

Numbers 15:32 In the wilderness the man gathered sticks upon the day.

I Samuel 4:12 And there ran a man of Benjamin, with earth upon his head.

I Samuel 14:11 Philistines, the come forth out of the holes where they had hid themselves.

Numbers 15:33 Him gathering sticks brought him to all the.

Numbers 31:20 Things made of wood.

SKIPPING GRAY MONITORS

Genesis 36:6 And Esau took his, all the persons of his house, and his cattle, and all his beasts, and went into the country from the face of his brother Jacob.

Genesis 36:7 They might dwell together: the land wherein they were strangers, because of their cattle.

Genesis 36:8 Thus dwelt Esau in mount, Esau is Edom.

Judges 11:17 The king of Edom would not hearken thereto. He would not consent: and abode.

Genesis 33:17 And Jacob built him a house, and made booths for his cattle.

Leviticus 23:42 Ye shall dwell in booths, all that are Israelites born, shall dwell in booths.

Genesis 37:1 Jacob dwelt in the land wherein his father was.

Lords People

Lords' words: Joseph was in Egypt, he proved himself, he was in prison and had much time to connect with lord. He became our shepherd of which others followed. This story is about our people then.

Joshua 17:17 Of Joseph, thou people, thou shalt have one only.

II Samuel 14:27 Woman fair.

Solomon 4:7 Thou art all fair, there is no spot in thee.

Solomon 5:12 His eyes are as the eyes of doves by the rivers of waters, and fitly set.

Solomon 5:14 His hands are gold: his belly is as bright ivory.

Job 1:10 Thou hast blessed the work of his hands, and his substance is increased in the land.

Job 1:12 All that he hath is in, only upon himself, and the presence of lord.

St. John 10:30 I and my father are one.

Job 2:5 He will curse thee to thy face.

Job 12:20 He removeth away the speech, the understanding of the aged.

Job 15:12 Doth thine heart carry and what do thy eyes wink at?

Job 22:27 Thou shalt make thy prayer unto him, and he shall hear thee.

Job 22:28 And the light shall shine upon thy ways.

Job 22:29 When men are cast down, then thou shalt say, there is lifting up: and he shall save the humble person.

Job 22:30 He shall deliver the island of the innocent: and it is delivered by the pureness of thine hands.

Tobit 13:14 Blessed are they which love thee, for they shall rejoice in thy peace: when they have seen all thy glory, and shall be glad for ever.

Leviticus 15:18 The woman also with whom man shall lie with seed of copulation.

Leviticus 19:31 Regard them that have familiar spirits.

SKIPPING GRAY MONITORS

Genesis 6:2 The sons, said the daughters, that they were fair, and they took them all which they chose.

Leviticus 12:2 If a woman have conceived seed, a man, then she shall be, seven days; for her firmity, shall she be clean.

Lords' words: If you choose to have sex with a woman, you spend seven days with her so that the seed of copulation has time to leave her, she then has time to choose to stay or leave. This allows for a non-codependent way of living and a peaceable mutual departure and experience.

Tobit 13:10 Give praise to lord, for he is good: and let him make joyful there in thee, and love in thee forever those that are miserable.

Sirach 13:25 The heart of a man changeth his countenance, whether it be for good or evil: and a merry heart maketh a cheerful countenance.

Sirach 13:26 A cheerful countenance is a token of a heart that is in prosperity.

Sirach 26:14 A silent and loving woman is a gift of lord.

Proverbs 6:25 Lust after her beauty in thine heart.

Proverbs 5:19 Let her be as the loving hind and pleasant roe, let her breasts satisfy thee all the times, and be thou ravished always with her love.

Lords' words: Some of Jacob's children were not upright humans.

Leviticus 12:4 She shall then continue in the, her purifying three and thirty days: she shall touch hallowed thing, until the days of her purifying be fulfilled.

Leviticus 12:5 The bare a child.

Deuteronomy 25:15 Thou shalt have a perfect and just weight, a perfect and just measure shalt thou have: that thy days may be lengthened in the land which lord giveth thee.

Isaiah 19:22 And lord shall heal them.

Isaiah 19:25 Whom lord shall bless, saying, blessed be Egypt my people, the work of my hands, mine inheritance.

TRUST 1 LORD

Genesis 47:6 The land of Egypt is before thee: If thou knowest any men of activity among them.

Nehemiah 4:6 For the people had a mind to work.

Isaiah 22:23 He shall be for a glorious throne to his father's house.

Deuteronomy 29:4 Lord hath given you a heart to perceive, and eyes to see, and ears to hear, unto this day.

Philippians 3:13 Brethren, I count not myself to have apprehended: but this one thing I do, forget those things which are behind, and reach forth to those things which are before.

I Corinthians 3:8 He that planteth, he that watereth, every man shall receive his own reward according to his own labor.

St. Luke 8:15 But that on the good ground, are they, which in an honest and good heart having heard the word, keep it, and bring forth fruit with patience.

II Corinthians 9:6 He which soweth sparingly, shall reap also sparingly: and he which soweth bountifully, shall reap also bountifully.

St. Luke 17:35 Two women shall be grinding together,

St. Luke 17:36 two men shall be in the field.

St. Mark 2:27 The sabbath was made for man.

Ecclesiastes 1:4 One generation passeth away, and another generation cometh: but the earth abideth forever.

II Samuel 7:3 Go, do all that is in thine heart: for lord is with thee.

II Esdras 3:8 And every people walked after their own will, and did wonderful things before thee.

II Corinthians 9:7 Every man according as he purposeth in his heart, so let him give; not grudgingly, or of necessity: for lord loveth a cheerful giver.

Ecclesiastes 2:24 There is nothing better than eat and drink, and that his soul enjoy good in his labor.

Ecclesiastes 3:1 To everything there is a season, and a time to every purpose under the heaven.

SKIPPING GRAY MONITORS

Ecclesiastes 3:2 A time to be born, a time to plant, and a time to pluck up that which is planted.

Ecclesiastes 3:3 A time to heal: and a time to build up.

Ecclesiastes 3:4 A time to laugh: and a time to dance.

Ecclesiastes 3:5 A time to cast stones, and a time to gather stones together: a time to embrace, and a time to refrain.

Ecclesiastes 3:13 Also that every man should eat and drink, and enjoy the good of all his labor: it is the gift of lord.

Ecclesiastes 8:8 There is no man that hath power over the spirit to retain the spirit; neither hath he power in the day of death: neither wickedness.

Ecclesiastes 8:15 A man hath no better thing under the sun, than to eat, and to drink, and to be merry: the days of his life, under the sun.

Deuteronomy 15:4 There shall be no poor among you.

St. John 8:33 Ye shall be made free.

II Corinthians 9:10 Bread for your food, multiply your seed sown, and increase the fruits of your righteousness.

Ezekiel 16:27 Behold, I have stretched out my hand over thee, and have diminished thine ordinary food.

St. Matthew 6:25 Therefore I say to you, take thought for your life, what ye shall eat, or what ye shall drink, for your body.

Leviticus 23:22 And when ye reap the harvest of your land, thou shalt not make clean riddance of the corners of thy field when thou reapest, neither shalt thou gather any gleaning of thy harvest: thou shalt leave them unto the poor, and to the stranger: I am lord.

Ezekiel 36:10 Wastes shall be ded.

Joshua 14:10 The children of wandered in the wilderness: and now, lo, this day.

Numbers 23:9 For from the top of the rocks I see him, and from the hills I behold him: lo, the people shall dwell alone.

Lords' words: Our people lived a wonderful peaceful life together understanding lord at every task, lords voice taught one way to each soul.

TRUST 1 LORD

St. Matthew 5:48 Be ye therefore perfect, as your father, which is in heaven, is perfect.

St. Matthew 22:37 Thou shalt love lord with all thy heart.

St. Matthew 19:18 Thou shalt do no murder.

St. Matthew 23:9 Call no man your father upon the earth: for 1 is your father, which is in heaven.

Malachi 3:6 For I am, lord, I change not.

Proverbs 6:17 A proud look.

Proverbs 6:23 Instruction are the way of life.

Proverbs 6:24 To keep thee from the evil, from the flattery of the tongue.

Proverbs 9:9 Give instruction to a wise man, and he will be yet wiser: teach a just man, and he will increase in learning.

Ecclesiastes 2:1 Enjoy pleasure.

Proverbs 9:17 Bread eaten in secret is pleasant.

Jeremiah 29:5 Build ye houses and dwell in them, and plant gardens, and eat the fruit of them.

Genesis 11:3 let us make brick, and burn them throughly. And they had brick for stone, and slime had they for mortar.

I Thessalonians 4:11 Study to be quiet, do your own business, work with your own hands, (as we command you:).

Acts of the Apostles 24:2 By thee we enjoy great quietness, and very worthy deeds are done unto this nation.

Acts of the Apostles 24:3 We accept it always, and in all places.

I Timothy 2:2 For all that are in authority; that we may lead a quiet and peaceable life and honesty.

I Thessalonians 4:13 Brethren, concerning them which are asleep, that ye sorrow not.

Sirach 4:22 Accept no person against thy soul, and let not the reverence of any man cause thee to fail:

Sirach 4:23 and refrain speak, when there is occasion to do good, and hide thy wisdom.

SKIPPING GRAY MONITORS

Sirach 4:27 Make not thy self an underling to a foolish man.

Psalms 91:1 He that dwelleth in the secret place of the most High: shall abide under the shadow of the Almighty.

Psalms 91:2 I will say of lord, He is my refuge, and my fortress: in him will I trust.

Psalms 92:1 It is a good thing to give thanks to lord, and to sing praises to thy name, O most high:

Psalms 92:2 to shew forth thy loving kindness in the morning: and thy faithfulness every night.

Psalms 21:13 So will we sing, and praise thy power.

Psalms 95:6 O come, let us worship and bow down: let us kneel before lord our maker.

Psalms 95:7 For he is our God, and we are the people of his pasture, and the sheep of his hand: To-day if ye will hear his voice.

Psalms 96:1 Sing to lord a new song: sing unto lord all the earth.

Psalms 105:6 Ye seed of Abraham his servant: ye children of Jacob his chosen.

Isaiah 26:7 The way of the just is uprightness.

Isaiah 30:7 For the Egyptians: their strength is to sit still.

Deuteronomy 26:5 Egypt became there a nation, great, mighty, and populous.

Exodus 40:36 The children of Israel went onward in all their journeys.

Tobit 14:4 Our brethren shall lie scattered in the earth from that good land.

Numbers 22:11 Behold, there is a people come out of Egypt, which covereth the face of the earth.

Numbers 23:10 Who can count the dust of Jacob.

The Ark

Lords' words: All Jacobs children are together with Issac and Abraham in Egypt. Giants built the pyramids at this time; they were our homes. Then we built them all over the world, each man to his own design.

Hebrews 11:8 By faith Abraham when he was called to go out into a place, obeyed, and he went out, not knowing.

Hebrews 11:7 By faith being warned of things not seen as yet, prepared an ark to the saving of his house, and became heir of the righteousness which is by faith.

Exodus 9:5 Lord shall do this thing in the land.

Joshua 3:14 The ark before the people;

Joshua 3:15 Jordan overfloweth all his banks at the time of.

Exodus 9:14 Thy people; there is none like me in all the earth.

I kings 8:21 And I have set there a place for the ark of lord, which he made with our fathers, the land of Egypt.

II Esdras 6:43 For as soon as thy word went forth, the work was made.

I Chronicles 22:2 Masons hew wrought stones to build the house of lord.

Ezra 3:7 They gave money also unto the masons, and to the carpenters.

I Chronicles 22:15 Moreover there are workmen with thee in abundance, hewers and workers of stone and timber, and all manner of cunning men for every manner of work.

I Chronicles 22:19 The ark, the house that is to be built to the name of lord.

I Samuel 6:1 The ark of lord was in the country.

II Chronicles 7:21 This house, which is high, shall be an astonishment to everyone that passeth by it, so that he shall say; why hath lord done thus to this land, and unto this house.

SKIPPING GRAY MONITORS

I kings 8:43 Hear thou, heaven thy dwelling place. All people of earth may know thy name, and they may know that this house which have builded, is called by thy name.

Deuteronomy 31:25 The ark of lord,

Deuteronomy 31:26 the side of the ark, that it may be there for a witness.

Joshua 3:17 The ark stood firm on dry ground.

Joshua 4:9 The ark of the stood: and they are there unto this day.

Ezekiel 28:13 Eden the garden, gold: the workmanship of thee.

Hebrews 9:4 The golden Censer, the ark laid roundabout with gold, wherein was the golden pot that had manna, and rod that budded,

Revelation 1:20 seven golden candlesticks.

I Esdras 8:11 As many therefore as have a mind thereunto, my seven friends the counselors.

Hebrews 11:9 Dwelling with Isaac and Jacob, the heirs with him of the same.

II Esdras 6:49 Then didst thou ordain two living creatures, one thou called Enoch.

Exodus 3:18 They shall hearken to thy voice: and thou shalt come, thou and the elders of Israel to Egypt.

Psalms 145:4 One generation shall praise thy works to another, an shall declare thy mighty acts.

Psalms 145:18 The lord is nigh unto all them that call upon him: to all that call upon him in truth.

Psalms 146:8 The lord loveth the righteous.

Psalms 148:7 Praise lord from the earth: ye dragons and all deeps.

Genesis 7:1 Lord said, come thou and all thy house into the ark: for thee have I seen righteous before me, in this generation.

Genesis 7:15 And they went in to the ark, wherein is the breath of life.

Genesis 7:16 They that went in of all flesh, as lord had commanded, and lord shut them in.

TRUST 1 LORD

St. Matthew 24:38 For as in the days that were, they were eating and drinking, marry and giving, that entered to the ark.

St. Matthew 24:39 Not until the flood came, the coming of man.

Hebrews 2:3 Which at the first began to be spoken by lord, and was confirmed unto us by them that heard him.

Proverbs 30:4 Who hath up in heaven, descended? In fist. Who hath bound the waters in a garm? Who hath established all the ends of the earth? What is his name, and what is his sons name, if thou canst tell?

Judah

Genesis 38:1 Judah went down from his brethren.

Genesis 11:4 They said: Go to, let us build us a city and a tower, and let us make us a name, lest we be scattered abroad.

Joshua 18:5 Judah abide in their coast on the south, and the house of Joseph abide in their coasts on the north.

I kings 4:20 Judah were many in multitude.

I kings 4:24 For he had dominion over all the region on side of the river.

I kings 4:31 For he was wiser than all men; his fame was all round about.

I kings 4:32 And he spake.

I kings 4:34 And there came all people to hear the wisdom.

Joshua 19:9 Of the children of Judah, the children of Simeon: for the part of the children of Judah was too much for them: therefore, the children of Simeon had their within them.

I kings 6:7 And the house was built of stone, made ready before it was brought thither: there was neither hammer nor axe nor any tool.

Numbers 24:21 Strong is thy dwelling place, thou puttest thy nest in a rock.

I kings 6:29 And he carved all the walls of the house roundabout with carved figures within & out.

I kings 6:36 And he built inner court with stone.

I kings 7:29 Were Lyons, there was a base beneath the Lyons, were of thin work.

I kings 7:34 And there were four corners of one base: the base itself.

I kings 7:36 For on the thereof, he graved lions, according to the proportion of every one round about.

I kings 7:37 After this manner he made the ten bases: all of them had one casting, one measure, and one size.

I kings 7:41 To cover which were upon the top of pillars.

TRUST 1 LORD

Tobit 13:16 For Jerusalem shall be built up with Emeralds: thy walls and towers, and battlements with pure gold.

I kings 8:13 I have surely built thee a house to dwell in, for thee to abide in forever.

I kings 8:49 Maintain their cause.

Deuteronomy 33:7 Judah, hear lord, the voice of. Let his hands be sufficient for him, and be thou a help to him from his enemies.

I kings 8:54 Kneeling on his knees, with his hands.

I kings 19:9 He lodged there.

I kings 11:38 My statues and my commandments.

I kings 12:20 And made him king over all, Judah only.

Genesis 19:20 Behold now, this city is near to flee unto, and it is a little one: Oh, let me escape thither, (is it not a little one?) and my fowl shall live.

Leviticus 12:6 The shall bring a lamb, a pigeon, or a turtledove, unto the.

Leviticus 12:8 And if the be not able to bring a lamb, then the shall bring two turtles, or two young pigeons.

Leviticus 11:15 Every raven after his kind.

Solomon 1:5 I am black, (O ye daughters of Jerusalem) as the tents of, as the curtains of.

Solomon 1:6 I am black, because the sun hath looked upon me.

Solomon 1:10 Thy cheeks are comely with rows of jewels, thy neck with chains of gold.

Solomon 4:3 Thy speech.

Solomon 5:11 His locks are bushy, and black as a Raven.

Solomon 5:15 His legs are as pillars of marble.

Solomon 7:5 Thine head upon thee is like Carmel, and the hair of thine head like purple.

II Esdras 12:31 And the Lyon whom rising up out of the wood, and roaring, and speaking to the Eagle.

SKIPPING GRAY MONITORS

Lords' words: Judah breed birds, sheep, humans, snakes, lions, all types of monsters.

II Samuel 1:23 They were swifter than eagles, they were stronger than Lions.

II Esdras 12:33 For he shall let them before him aline in judgment, and shall rebuke them and correct them.

Proverbs 30:25 The ants are a people not strong, yet they prepare their meat in the summer.

Tobit 6:2 And when the young went down to wash himself, a fish leaped out of the river, and would devour.

Tobit 6:14 Wicked spirit loveth, which hurteth body.

Jeremiah 50:39 The wild beasts of the desert with the wild beasts of the islands shall dwell there, from generation to generation.

Jeremiah 51:37 A dwelling place for dragons.

Jeremiah 51:38 They shall roar together, lions.

II Chronicles 19:1 Judah returned to his house in peace to Jerusalem.

Numbers 24:9 He couched, he lay down as a Lion, and as a great Lion: who shalt stir him up? Blessed is he that blessed thee, and cursed is he that curseth thee.

Ezekiel 19:2 What is thy mother? A lioness: thee lay down among lions, the nourished her whelps among young lions.

Ezekiel 19:3 Young lion, it learned to catch the prey, and devoured men.

Job 4:10 The roaring of the Lyon, and the voice of the fierce Lyon, and the teeth of the young Lyons, are.

Isaiah 65:4 The which eat swine's flesh, abominable thing.

Isaiah 66:3 He that killeth an ox is as if he slew a man; a lamb, a dog, swine. They have chosen their own ways, and the soul in there.

St. Mark 3:30 He hath an unclean spirit.

II Esdras 3:22 The good departed away, and the evil abode still.

Sirach 9:13 Keep the far from the man that hath power to kill, and if thou come unto him, make no fault, least he take away thy life presently.

TRUST 1 LORD

Tobit 12:10 They that sin are enemies to their life.

Sirach 7:6 Lay a stumbling block in the way.

St. Matthew 8:16 Many were possessed with spirits.

II Esdras 6:37 For my spirit was greatly set on fire, my soul.

St. Matthew 12:45 Then goeth he, and taketh with himself other spirits more wicked than himself, and they enter in and dwell there: and the last state of that man is worse than the first. Even so shall it be also unto the wicked generation.

St. Matthew 23:15 Woe unto you: and when he is made, ye make him two-fold more the child of hell than yourselves.

Sirach 6:4 A wicked soul shall destroy him that hath it.

St. Matthew 17:15 He is lunatic.

St. Matthew 23:33 Ye serpents, ye generation of vipers.

St. Matthew 24:10 And then shall many betray one another, and shall hate one another.

St. Matthew 24:11 And many shall deceive.

St. Matthew 24:12 The love of many wax cold.

Numbers 23:24 Behold, the people shall rise up as a great Lyon, and lift up himself as a young lion: he shall not lie down until he eat of the prey, the slain.

St. Matthew 18:7 Woe unto the world because of offenses.

II Esdras 4:20 Thou hast given a right judgment, but why judgest thou not thy self also?

St. Mark 2:8 They reason within themselves. Why reason ye these things in your hearts?

Sirach 7:8 Build not one sin upon another.

II kings 14:10 And tarry at home: for why shouldest thou meddle to thy hurt, that thou shouldest fall, thou, Judah.

Job 6:6 An egg?

Job 6:7 The things that my soul refused to touch, my sorrowful meat.

Isaiah 59:5 He that eateth eggs dieth.

SKIPPING GRAY MONITORS

Job 4:11 The old Lyon perisheth for lack of prey, and the stout Lyon's whelps are scattered abroad.

Job 5:3 I have seen the foolish taking root: but suddenly I cursed his habitation.

Job 5:7 Yet man is born unto trouble, as the sparks fly upward.

Isaiah 22:11 Ye have not looked to the maker thereof, neither had respect to him that fashioned it long ago.

II Esdras 7:24 But his law have they despised, and denied: not been faithful, and not performed his works.

II Maccabees 11:4 Not at all considering the power of lord.

Job 14:21 His sons come to honor, and he knoweth it; and they are brought low, but he perceiveth it not of them.

Job 6:25 How forcible are right words? What doeth your arguing reprove?

Job 14:19 Thou destroyest the hope of man.

Job 19:2 How long will ye vex my soul, and break me in pieces with words?

Job 30:28 I went mourning without the sun: I stood up, and I cried.

Job 23:13 He is in one mind, and who can turn him? And what his soul desireth, even that he doeth.

Job 23:14 For he performeth the thing that is appointed for me: and many such things are with him.

Job 23:15 Therefore am I troubled at his presence:

Job 23:16 the Almighty troubleth.

I Chronicles 9:3 In Jerusalem dwelt of the children of Judah, and of the children of Benjamin, and of the children of Ephraim, and Manasseh.

Ezra 9:1 The people have separated themselves from the, doing according to their abominations.

Psalms 81:5 This he ordained in Joseph for a testimony, when he went out through the land of Egypt: where I heard a language, that I understood not.

TRUST 1 LORD

Psalms 106:35 Were mingled among the heathen, and learned their works.

Ezekiel 7:3 I will judge thee according to thy ways,

I kings 9:3 and mine eyes and mine heart shall be there perpetually.

Ezekiel 8:11 Of the ancients of the house of Israel, with every man his censer in his hand, and a thick cloud of incense went up.

Ezekiel 8:17 The house of Judah, they commit abominations, for they have filled the land with violence, and have returned to provoke me to anger.

Esther 11:7 Nation were prepared to battle, that they might fight against the righteous people.

I kings 12:21 And come to Jerusalem, all the house of Judah, with the tribe of Benjamin, which were to fight against the house of Israel.

II Chronicles 11:1 Jerusalem, of the house of Judah and Benjamin and chosen men, which were to fight against Israel.

I kings 12:24 Thus saith lord, ye shall not go up, nor fight against your brethren the children of Israel: return every man to his house, for this thing is from me. They hearkened therefore to the word of lord, and returned to depart, according to the word of lord.

II Chronicles 11:4 Thus saith lord, Ye shall not go up, nor fight against your brethren: return every man to his house, for this thing is done of me. And they obeyed the words of lord, and returned from going against.

I Samuel 4:3 The ark of lord, when it cometh us, it save us out of the hand of our enemies.

Psalms 21:11 For they intended evil against thee: they imagined a mischievous devise, which they are not able to perform.

I kings 13:33 After this thing returned not from his evil way.

I kings 16:21 Then the people of Israel divided into two parts: half of the people followed king.

I kings 18:6 So they divided the land between them to pass throughout it.

SKIPPING GRAY MONITORS

II Chronicles 16:1 Judah, to the intent that he might let none go out or come in, of Judah.

II Esdras 2:22 Keep the old and young within the walls.

I kings 18:40 And let not one of them escape. They took them and slew them there.

Job 3:16 infants which never saw light.

II Samuel 19:43 The words of the men of Judah were fiercer than the words of the men of.

II Samuel 20:2 The men of Judah,

II Samuel 20:3 took the women whom he had to keep the house, and put them in ward, and fed them, but went not in unto them: so, they were shut up unto the day of their death, living in widowhood.

Esther 2:8 Many maidens were gathered together. The palace, keeper of the women.

Esther 2:9 And the maiden pleased him, and she obtained kindness of him, and seven maidens, which were meet to be given out of the house, and he preferred her and her maids, the best of the house of the women.

Esther 2:17 All virgins.

Job 3:18 There the prisoners rest together, they hear the voice of the oppressor.

Job 3:23 Why is light given to a man?

Job 4:7 Who ever perished, being innocent? Where were he righteous cut off?

Esther 7:4 For we are sold, I and my people, to be destroyed, to be slain, and to perish: Bondmen, and bondwomen, I had held my tongue, the kings damage.

I Esdras 4:59 From thee cometh wifedom, I am thy servant.

Sirach 43:33 To the godly hath he given wife-dome.

Sirach 36:24 He that getteth a wife, beginneth a possession.

I kings 19:10 And have been very jealous for the life to take it away.

Esther 1:17 All women, they shall despise their husbands in their eyes, when it shall be reported.

TRUST 1 LORD

Sirach 31:13 Remember that a wicked eye is an evil thing: upon every occasion.

Proverbs 5:1 My son, attend to my wisdom, and bow thine ear to my understanding.

Proverbs 5:2 That thou mayest regard discretion, and that thy lips may keep knowledge.

Sirach 28:13 Curse the whisperer, and the double tongued: for such have destroyed many that were at peace.

Wisdom of Solomon 1:10 For the ear of jealousy heareth all things: and the noise of murmurings is not hid.

Proverbs 5:3 For the lips drop as a honeycomb, and mouth is smoother than oil.

Wisdom of Solomon 1:11 Therefore beware of murmuring, which is unprofitable; and refrain your tongue from backbiting: for there is no word so secret that shall go for naught: and the mouth that lieth slayeth the soul.

Proverbs 5:4 But end is bitter, as sharp as a two-edged sword.

Proverbs 5:5 Feet go down to death, steps take hold.

Proverbs 5:6 Thou canst know them.

Proverbs 9:14 For she sitteth at the door of her house, in the high places of the city.

Proverbs 9:18 But he knoweth not that the dead are there, and that her guests are in the depths of hell.

Sirach 25:16 Rather dwell with a Lyon, a dragon, then to keep house with a wicked woman.

Sirach 25:17 The wickedness of a woman changeth her face, and darkeneth her countenance.

Sirach 25:23 A woman that will not comfort.

Sirach 25:26 Let her go.

Proverbs 5:7 Hear me now therefore, O ye children: depart not from the words of my mouth.

SKIPPING GRAY MONITORS

Proverbs 5:8 Remove thy way far from, and come not nigh the door of house.

Proverbs 5:9 Lest thou give thine honor unto others, and thy years unto the cruel:

Proverbs 5:10 lest strangers be filled with thy wealth, and thy labors be in the house of a stranger,

Proverbs 5:11 and thou mourn at the last, when thy flesh and thy body are consumed,

Proverbs 5:12 and say, how have I hated instruction, and my heart despised reproof?

Proverbs 5:13 And have not obeyed the voice of my teacher, nor inclined mine ear?

Proverbs 5:14 I was almost in all evil, in the midst of the congregation & assembly.

Ezra 10:11 Lord your father, do his pleasure: and separate yourselves from the people of the land, and from the strange wives.

Psalms 53:5 There were they in great fear, where no fear was.

Wisdom of Solomon 1:12 Seek not death in the error of your life: and pull not upon your selves destruction.

Psalms 57:4 My soul is among Lyons: and I lie even among them, the men, whose teeth are spears and arrows, and their tongue a sharp sword.

Proverbs 19:12 The king's wrath is the roaring of a Lyon.

Psalms 60:7 Judah is law.

I Esdras 3:5 Let every one of us speak a sentence: he that shall overcome, a whole sentence shall seem wiser than the others, unto him shall the king give great gifts, and great things in token of victory.

I Esdras 4:3 King is more mighty: for he is lord of all these things, and hath dominion over them, and whatsoever he commandeth them, they do.

I kings 21:29 Seest thou how himself before me? Because he himself before me, I will not bring the evil in his days: but in his son's days will I bring the evil upon his house.

TRUST 1 LORD

I kings 19:3 Life, which belongeth to Judah, his servant there.

I Esdras 4:4 If he bid them make war the one against the other, they do it: if he send them out against the enemies, they go, and break down mountains, walls and towers.

I Esdras 4:5 They slay and are slain, and transgress not the king's commandment: if they get victory, they bring all to the king, as well the spoil as all things else.

I Esdras 4:7 Yet he is but one man; if he command to kill, they kill, if he command to spare, they spare.

I Esdras 4:8 If he command to smite, they smite; if he command to make desolate, they make desolate; if he command to build, they build:

I Esdras 4:9 if he command to cut down, they cut down; if he command to plant, they plant.

I Esdras 4:10 So all his people and his armies obey him; furthermore, he lieth down, he eateth and drinketh, and taketh his rest.

I Esdras 4:11 And these keep (watch) round about him, neither may any one depart, and do his own business, neither disobey they him in anything.

I Esdras 4:12 Ye men, be mightiest when he is obeyed.

Proverbs 22:7 The rich ruleth over the poor, and the borrower is servant to the lender.

II kings 9:17 Take a horseman, and send to meet them, and let him say, is.

Tobit 9:4 If I Tarry long, he will be very sorry.

I Esdras 1:16 Moreover the porters were at every gate: it was not lawful for any to go from his ordinary service: for their brethren prepared for them.

II kings 4:43 He said, the people, they may eat: They shall eat, and shall thereof.

I kings 19:7 Arise, and eat, because the journey is too great for thee.

II kings 4:44 So he set it before them, and they did eat.

II kings 7:10 There was no man there, neither voice of man, but horses tied, and asses tied.

II kings 8:9 Camels' burden.

Ezekiel 12:18 Son, eat thy bread with quaking, and drink thy water with trembling and with carefulness.

Psalms 106:20 Thus they changed their glory, into the similitude of an ox that eateth grass.

II Esdras 4:12 We should live still in wickedness, and to suffer, and to know.

Nehemiah 8:17 Captivity made.

Nehemiah 13:3 All the mixed multitude.

Isaiah 45:13 Let go my captives, saith lord.

II kings 10:24 Letteth go, his life shall be for the life of him.

I Esdras 2:22 And shalt understand that that city was rebellious, troubling kings and cities.

I Esdras 2:23 And that the Jews were rebellious, and railed always wars therein, for the which cause even this city was made desolate.

I Esdras 2:27 The men therein were given to rebellion, and war, and that mighty fierce were in Jerusalem, who reigned and exacted tributes.

Lamentations 2:15 They hiss and wag their head at the, of Jerusalem.

Lamentations 2:16 They hiss and gnash the teeth: they have swallowed up: we have seen it.

Lamentations 2:21 The young and the old lye on the ground in the streets.

I Esdras 4:45 The Edomites burnt Judea.

I Esdras 4:53 Have free liberty as well.

I Esdras 4:62 He hath given them freedom and liberty.

II kings 14:19 Now they made a conspiracy.

Exodus 38:4 And he made for the a network, under thereof, beneath unto the midst of it.

Isaiah 48:1 Of Judah, which swear by the name of lord, and make mention of the God of Israel, but not in truth.

TRUST 1 LORD

Romans 1:25 Who changed the truth of God to a lie, and worshipped and served the creature.

Isaiah 57:8 Behind the doors the hast set up thy remembrance: another than me, and art gone up: thou hast enlarged and made the a covenant with it.

Wisdom of Solomon 12:24 For they went astray very far in the ways of error, & held them for gods (amongst the beasts) being deceived as children of no understanding.

Wisdom of Solomon 13:1 Surely vain are all men by nature, who are ignorant of lord, and could not out of the good things that are seen, know him that is: neither by considering the works, did they acknowledge the work-master.

Wisdom of Solomon 13:2 But deemed either fire, or wind, or the swift air, or the circle of the stars, or the violent water, or the lights of heaven to be the gods which govern the world.

II Esdras 7:23 And deceived themselves by their wicked deeds, and said of the most high, that he is not, and knew not his ways.

Wisdom of Solomon 13:6 for they err seeking God, and desirous to find him.

St. Matthew 6:24 No man can serve two masters: ye cannot serve God.

Wisdom of Solomon 13:9 For if they were able to know so much, that they could aim at the world; how did they not sooner find out the lord thereof?

Deuteronomy 31:27 For I know thy rebellion, and thy stiff neck: behold, I am alive with you this day, ye have been rebellious against lord.

Nehemiah 8:1 And all the people gathered themselves together as one, and they spake the law of which commanded to,

Nehemiah 8:2 all that could hear with understanding.

II Chronicles 17:9 And they taught in Judah, and had the book of the law with them, and went about throughout all the cities of Judah, and taught the people.

SKIPPING GRAY MONITORS

Nehemiah 8:3 And he read therein before the street that was before the water, from morning until midday, before the men and the women, and those that could understand: and the ears of all the people were attentive unto the book of the law.

Nehemiah 8:4 The stood upon a pulpit of wood, which they had made for the purpose, and beside him stood on his right hand: and on his left hand.

Nehemiah 8:7 The caused the people to understand the law: and the people stood in their place.

I Esdras 5:37 Neither could they shew their families, nor their stock, how they were of Israel.

I Esdras 5:39 And when the description of the kindred of these men was sought in the Register, and was not found, they were removed, executing the.

II Maccabees 6:6 Neither was it lawful for a man to keep sabbath days.

Nehemiah 8:11 So the stilled all the people, saying, hold your peace, for the day is holy, neither be ye grieved.

II kings 23:2 All the of Judah, and all the inhabitants of with him, and all the people, both small and great: in their ears all the words of he.

St. Matthew 6:7 For they think that they shall be heard for their much speaking.

Wisdom of Solomon 14:12 for the devising of idols was the beginning of spiritual fornication, and the invention of them the corruption of life.

Wisdom of Solomon 14:13 For neither were they from the beginning, neither shall they be forever.

Wisdom of Solomon 14:15 For a father afflicted with untimely mourning, when he hath made an image of his child soon taken away, now honored him as a god, which was then a dead man, and delivered to those that were under him ceremonies and sacrifices.

TRUST 1 LORD

Wisdom of Solomon 14:16 Thus in process of time an ungodly custom grown strong was kept as a law, and graven images were worshiped by the commandments of the kings,

Wisdom of Solomon 14:17 whom men could not honor in presence, because they dwelt far off, they took the counterfeit of his visage from far, and made an express image of a king whom they honored, to the end that by this their forwardness, they might flatter him that was absent, as if he were present.

Wisdom of Solomon 14:18 Also the singular diligence of the artificer did help to set forward the ignorant to more superstition.

Wisdom of Solomon 14:19 For he, peradventure willing to please one in authority, forced all his skill to make the resemblance of the best fashion.

Wisdom of Solomon 14:20 And so the multitude allured by the grace of the work, took him now for a god, which a little before was but honored as a man.

Wisdom of Solomon 14:22 Moreover this was not enough for them, that they erred in the knowledge of lord, but whereas they lived in the great war of ignorance, those so great plagues called they peace.

Wisdom of Solomon 14:23 For whilst they slew their children in sacrifices, or used secret ceremonies, or made revealing's of strange rites.

Wisdom of Solomon 14:24 They kept neither lives nor marriages any longer undefiled: but either one slew another traitorously, or grieved him by adultery.

Wisdom of Solomon 14:29 For insomuch as their trust is in idols which have no life, though they swear falsely, yet they look not to be hurt.

Wisdom of Solomon 14:30 Howbeit for causes shall they be justly punished: both because they thought not well of lord, giving heed unto idols, and also unjustly swore in deceit, despising holiness.

Wisdom of Solomon 15:3 For to know thee is perfect righteousness.

SKIPPING GRAY MONITORS

Wisdom of Solomon 15:11 Forasmuch as he knew not his maker, and him that inspired into him an active soul, and breathed in a living spirit.

Wisdom of Solomon 15:12 But they counted our life a pastime, & our time here a market for gain: for, say they, we must be getting every way, though it be by evil means.

Wisdom of Solomon 15:13 For this man that of earthly matter maketh graven images, knoweth himself to offend above all.

Wisdom of Solomon 15:14 And all the enemies of thy people, that hold them in subjection are most foolish and are more miserable then babes.

Wisdom of Solomon 15:16 For man made them, and he that borrowed his own spirit fashioned them, but no man can make a lord like unto himself.

Wisdom of Solomon 15:18 Yea they worshiped those beasts also that are most hateful: some are worse than others.

Wisdom of Solomon 15:19 They went without the praise of lord and his blessing.

Sirach 37:7 There is some that counselleth for himself.

Leviticus 7:20 The soul that eateth of the flesh of the sacrifice of peace offerings, that pertain unto lord, having his uncleanness upon him, even that soul shall be cut off from his people.

Wisdom of Solomon 17:8 For they that promised to drive away terrors, and troubles from a sick soul, were sick themselves of fear worthy to be laughed at.

Baruch 6:36 They can save no man from death.

II Chronicles 13:18 Thus the children of Israel were brought under at that time, the children of Judah, because they relied upon the God of their father.

Wisdom of Solomon 13:13 Those which served to no use.

Sirach 31:4 The poor laboureth in his poor estate, and when he leaveth off, he is still needy.

TRUST 1 LORD

Lords' words: Snakes, our mother is a snake and was always divinely guided, therefore lord has always healed the snake species, even crooked snakes. Judah was not happy with the snake species being healed, unlike his family, so he made everyone afraid of snakes.

Wisdom of Solomon 16:5 For when the horrible fierceness of beasts came upon these, and they perished with the stings of crooked serpents, thy wrath endured, forever.

Wisdom of Solomon 16:6 They were troubled, that they might be admonished, having a sign of salvation.

Wisdom of Solomon 16:8 And in this thou madest thine enemies confess, that it is thou who deliverest from all evil.

Wisdom of Solomon 16:10 But thy sons, teeth of venomous dragons overcame: for my mercy was ever by them, and healed them.

Wisdom of Solomon 16:11 For they remember thy words, and were quickly saved, that not falling into a deep forgetfulness, they might be continually mindful of thy goodness.

Wisdom of Solomon 16:12 That restored them to health: O lord, which heal all things.

Wisdom of Solomon 16:14 A man indeed kill through his malice: and the spirit when it is gone forth returneth not; the soul received up, cometh again.

Wisdom of Solomon 16:24 For the creature that serve thee who art the maker, increase his strength against the unrighteous.

Wisdom of Solomon 16:26 That thy children, O lord, whom thou love, might know that it is the growing of fruits that nourish man: it is thy word which preserve them that put their trust in thee.

Wisdom of Solomon 17:3 For while they supposed to lie hid in their secret sins, they were scattered under a dark veil of forgetfulness, being horribly astonished, and troubled with strange apparitions.

II Esdras 5:5 And the people shall be troubled.

II Esdras 9:3 Therefore when there shall be uproars of the people in the world.

SKIPPING GRAY MONITORS

St. Matthew 28:15 So they did as they were taught, among the Jews until this day.

Sirach 47:25 For they sought out all wickedness, till the vengeance came upon them.

Wisdom of Solomon 19:13 And punishments came upon the sinners not without former signs by the force of thunders: for they suffered justly, according to their own wickedness, insomuch as they used a more hard and hateful behavior toward strangers.

Galatians 5:26 Let us not be desirous of vain glory, provoking one another, envying one another.

II Esdras 5:9 And all friends shall destroy one another: then shall withdraw self into his chamber.

II Esdras 5:12 At the same time shall men hope, but nothing obtain: they shall labor, but their ways shall not prosper.

II Esdras 6:24 At that time shall friends fight one against another like enemies, and stand in fear with those that dwell therein, they shall run.

Isaiah 14:3 In the day that lord shall give thee sorrow, and fear, and hard bondage wherein thou wast made to serve.

Isaiah 16:10 And gladness is taken away, and joy. There shall be no singing, there shall be shouting: I have made their vintage shouting to cease.

Lamentations 1:13 From above hath he sent fire into my bones, and it prevaileth against the: he hath spread a net for my feet, he hath turned me back: he hath made me faint all day.

Lamentations 1:14 The yoke of my transgressions is bound by his hand: he hath made my strength to fail, lord hath. I am not able to rise up.

Isaiah 14:11 Thy is brought down to the grave.

Isaiah 14:16 They that see thee shall narrowly look upon thee, and consider thee, saying; Is this the man that made the earth to tremble that did make kingdoms?

TRUST 1 LORD

II Esdras 9:5 For like as all that is made in the world hath a beginning, and an end, and the end is manifest.

II Esdras 11:32 But this head put the whole earth in fear, and bare rule in it over all those that dwelt upon the earth, with much oppression, and it had the governance of the world more then all that had been.

II Esdras 11:45 Thy Malicious heads.

Wisdom of Solomon 1:5 Discipline will remove from thoughts that are without understanding: and will not abide when unrighteousness cometh in.

Maccabees 8:16 And they committed to one man every year, who ruled over all their country, and all were obedient to that one.

Isaiah 14:18 All the kings of the nation, all of them lie, everyone in his own.

Isaiah 14:26 This is the purpose that is purposed upon the whole earth:

Isaiah 14:27 who shall dis annul it?

Isaiah 18:2 To a people terrible from their beginning, meted out and trodden down;

Isaiah 18:3 all ye inhabitants of the world.

Isaiah 19:4 A cruel lord; a fierce king shall rule over them, saith lord.

II Esdras 1:6 Because the sins of their fathers are increased in them: for they have forgotten me, & have offered unto strange gods.

Sirach 18:23 Be not as one that tempteth lord.

Sirach 18:24 Think upon the wrath that shall be at the: and the time of vengeance when he shall turn away his face.

II Chronicles 20:4 And Judah gathered themselves together, to ask help of lord: even out of all the cities of Judah they came to seek lord.

St. Matthew 8:18 Now when Jesus saw great multitudes about him, he gave commandment to depart unto the other side.

St. Matthew 9:12 They that be whole need not a physician.

I Chronicles 21:3 Lord make his people a hundred times more as they be.

SKIPPING GRAY MONITORS

Ephesians 6:8 Knowing that whatsoever good thing any man doeth, the same shall he receive of lord, whether he be bond or free.

Flood

Lords' words: We have chosen to take out Judah. This time for good.

Esther 3:8 There is a certain people scattered abroad, and dispersed among the people, in all the provinces of thy kingdom, and their laws are diverse from all people, neither keep they laws: it is not for the to suffer them.

Esther 13:4 Throughout the world, there was scattered a certain malicious people, that had laws contrary to our kingdoms, intended by us, cannot go forward.

Genesis 6:11 The earth also was corrupt before lord; and the earth was filled with violence.

Esther 13:5 Seeing when we understand that this people alone is continually in opposition unto to all men, differing in the strange manner of their laws, and evil affected to our state, working all the mischief they can, that our kingdom may not be firmly established.

Psalms 21:8 Thine hand shall find out all thine enemies, thy right hand shall find out those that hate thee.

Genesis 41:54 Dearth was in all lands: but in all the land of Egypt there was bread.

Jeremiah 15:4 Manasseh, king of Judah, in Jerusalem.

Jeremiah 15:11 Lord said, verily it shall be well with thy, verily I will cause the enemy in the time of affliction.

Jeremiah 16:10 And it shall come to pass when thou shalt shew this people. This great evil against us? Or what is our iniquity? Our sin, that we have committed against lord.

Ezekiel 23:27 Thus will I make thy lewdness to cease from thee.

Jeremiah 16:21 The shall know that my name is Lord.

Jeremiah 17:4 For ye have kindled a fire in mine anger.

Jeremiah 17:5 Thus saith lord, cursed be the man that trusteth in man, and whose heart departeth from lord.

SKIPPING GRAY MONITORS

Jeremiah 17:23 They obeyed not, but made their neck stiff, that they might not hear nor receive instruction,

Jeremiah 17:24 diligently hearken to me, saith lord.

Ezekiel 33:20 Lord is not equal. I judge you every one after his ways.

Isaiah 24:17 Fear, & the snare, are upon thee, O inhabitant of the earth.

Isaiah 24:18 And it shall come to pass.

Isaiah 24:23 Lord shall reign before his ancients gloriously.

Isaiah 25:9 Lo, we have waited for him, and he will save us: this is the lord, we have waited for him, we will be glad, and rejoice in his salvation.

Isaiah 26:9 With my soul have I desired thee in the night, with my spirit within me will I seek thee early: for when thy judgments are in the earth, the inhabitants of the world will learn righteousness.

Isaiah 26:12 Lord, thou wilt ordain peace for us.

Isaiah 26:20 Come, my people, enter thou into thy chambers, and shut thy doors about thee; hide thy self as it were for a little moment, until the indignation be over past.

Isaiah 26:21 For behold, lord cometh out of his place to punish the inhabitants of the earth for their iniquity.

Isaiah 27:4 Fury is not in me: who would set the briers and thorns against me in battle? I would go through them, together.

Isaiah 27:5 Take hold of my strength, that may make peace with me, and shall make peace with me.

Isaiah 28:2 Behold, lord a mighty strong one, which as a destroying storm, shall cast down to the earth with the hand.

Isaiah 30:1 Woe to the rebellious children, saith lord, that take counsel, but not of me; and that cover with a covering, but not of my spirit, that they may add sin to sin.

Isaiah 30:2 That walk to go down into Egypt, (and have not asked at my mouth) to strengthen themselves in the strength of, and to trust in the, of Egypt.

Isaiah 30:3 Therefore shall the be your confusion.

TRUST 1 LORD

Isaiah 30:4 For his princes and his ambassadors,

Isaiah 30:5 they were all ashamed of a people that could not profit them, nor be a help nor profit, but a shame and also a reproach.

Isaiah 30:6 The burden of the beasts of the South: into the land of trouble and anguish, from whence come the young and old Lyon, the viper and serpent, they will carry their riches.

Isaiah 30:9 This is a rebellious people, lying children, children that will not hear.

Isaiah 30:10 Which say, prophesy not unto us right things: speak unto us smooth things, prophesy deceits.

Isaiah 30:11 The cause the holy One of Israel to cease from before us.

Exodus 9:15 For now I will stretch out my hand, that I may smite thee and thy people.

Exodus 9:18 Behold, to-morrow about this time I will cause it to rain a very grievous hail, such as hath not been in Egypt.

Exodus 9:19 Send therefore now, and gather thy cattle, and all that thou hast in the field: for upon every man and beast which that be found in the field, and that not be brought home, the hail shall come down upon them, and they shall die.

Exodus 9:21 And he that regarded not the word of lord, left his servants and his cattle in the field.

Exodus 9:23 Lord sent thunder and rained hail upon the land of Egypt.

Sirach 46:6 And with hailstones of mighty power he made the battle to fall violently upon the nation, that the nation might know all their strength, because he fought in the sight of lord, and he followed One.

Genesis 7:17 And the flood was upon the earth; and the waters increased, up above the earth.

Genesis 7:21 And all flesh died, both of fowl, of cattle, and of beast, and of every creeping thing that creepeth, and every man.

Exodus 9:29 The thunder shall cease, neither be any hail. That thou mayest know that the earth is lords.

Lords' words

Isaiah 45:5 I am lord, there is none else, there is no God beside me: I girded thee, though thou hast not known me:

Isaiah 45:6 that they may know from the rising of the sun, that there is none beside me. I am lord, and there is none else.

Isaiah 45:7 I form the light, and create darkness: I make peace, and create evil: I lord do all these things.

Isaiah 45:8 I lord have created it.

Isaiah 45:9 Woe unto him that striveth with his maker.

Isaiah 45:18 The earth, he hath established it, he formed it to be inhabited.

Isaiah 45:19 I lord speak righteousness; I declare things that are right.

Isaiah 45:23 Unto me every knee shall bow.

I Samuel 3:17 What is the thing that lord hath said to thee? I pray thee hide it from men.

Isaiah 52:5 Saith lord, my name continually every day is blasphemed.

Isaiah 52:6 Therefore people shall know my name: they shall know that I am he that doth speak. Behold, it is I.

Isaiah 52:7 How beautiful.

Isaiah 52:15 So shall he sprinkle many nations, for that which had not been told them, shall they see, and that which they had not heard, shall they consider.

Proverbs 8:34 Blessed is the man that heareth me:

Proverbs 8:35 for whoso findeth me, findeth life, and shall obtain favor of lord.

Proverbs 8:36 But he that sinneth against me, wrongeth his own soul; all they that hate me, love death.

Proverbs 9:10 The fear of lord is the beginning of understanding.

TRUST 1 LORD

Isaiah 54:8 In a little wrath I hid my face from thee, for a moment; but with everlasting kindness will I have mercy on thee, saith lord thy Redeemer.

St. John 4:23 The hour cometh, and now is, when the true worshippers shall worship Father in spirit, and in truth: for Father seeketh such to worship him.

Romans 13:11 And that, knowing the time, that now is high time to awake out of sleep: now is our salvation nearer then when we believed.

Isaiah 54:13 And all thy children shall be taught of lord, and great shall be the peace of thy children.

Isaiah 54:14 In righteousness shalt thou be established: thou shalt be far from oppression, for thou shalt not fear; for it shall not come near thee.

Isaiah 56:1 Thus saith lord, keep ye judgment, and do justice: my righteousness be revealed.

Isaiah 56:2 Blessed is the man that doeth this, and the son of man that layeth hold on it: that keepeth from polluting it, and keepeth his hand from doing any evil.

Isaiah 56:3 Let the son, the stranger, join himself to lord. Lord hath utterly separated me from people: Behold I am.

Isaiah 56:4 And choose the things that please me.

Isaiah 56:6 Also join selves to lord, to serve him, and to love the name of lord, to be his servants, every one, keepeth the sabbath, and taketh hold of.

Sirach 2:1 My son, if thou come to serve lord, prepare thy soul for temptation.

Sirach 2:2 Set thy heart aright, and constantly endure, and make not hast in time of trouble.

Sirach 2:3 Cleave unto him, and depart not away, that thou mayest be increased at thy last end.

Sirach 2:4 Whatsoever is brought upon thee, take cheerfully, and be patient when thou art changed to a low estate.

SKIPPING GRAY MONITORS

Tobit 13:2 He leadeth down to hell, and up again.

Tobit 13:6 Who can tell if he will accept you, and have mercy on you?

Sirach 2:6 Believe in him and he will help thee, order thy ways aright, and trust in him.

Sirach 5:3 And say not, who shall control me for my works: for lord will surely revenge thy pride.

Sirach 5:7 Make no tarrying to turn to lord, and put not off from day to day.

Sirach 6:18 My son, gather information from thy youth up: so shalt thou find wisdom till thine old age.

Sirach 6:23 Give ear, my son, receive my advice, and refuse not my counsel.

Sirach 7:14 Make not much babbling when thou prayest.

Sirach 8:10 Kindle not the coals of a sinner, lest thou be burnt with the flame of his fire.

Sirach 23:10 He that sweareth and nameth lord continually, shall not be faultless.

Sirach 23:28 It is great glory to follow lord, & to be received of him is long life.

Sirach 28:8 Abstain from strife and thou shalt diminish thy sins.

Sirach 30:21 Give not over thy mind to heaviness, and afflict not thy self in thine own counsel.

Sirach 32:8 Let thy speech be short, comprehending much in few words.

Sirach 34:9 A man that knoweth many things: he that hath much experience, will declare wisdom.

Sirach 36:11 All the tribes of Jacob together, inherit thou, as from the beginning.

Sirach 38:2 For of the most high cometh healing, and he shall receive honor of the king.

TRUST 1 LORD

Sirach 38:3 The skill of the shall lift up his head: and in the sight of great men he shall be in admiration.

Sirach 38:9 My son, in thy sickness be not negligent: but pray unto lord.

Sirach 38:24 The wisdom of a learned man cometh leisure; he shall become wise.

Sirach 38:34 They will maintain the state of the world, and all their desire is in the work of their craft.

Sirach 41:14 My children, keep discipline peace: for wisdom is hid, and a treasure.

Isaiah 58:3 Behold in the day of your fast ye find pleasure, and exact all your labors.

Sirach 31:20 Moderate eating.

Lords' words: Eat freshly ground healthy seed for flour, make bread or cook the seeds so they are soft. Eat fruits in their season and herbs in their season. Eat before 4:00 p.m. once a day. Think of how a snake eats, when they eat too much food they may not need to eat the next day to fully digest. Meat takes longer to digest. Listen to guidance, as all souls are different in their paths.

II Esdras 5:13 Fast seven days, thou shalt hear yet greater things.

II Esdras 5:22 And my soul recovered the spirit of understanding, and I began to talk with the most high again.

II Esdras 6:31 If thou wilt pray yet more, fast seven days again, I shall tell the greater things by day, then have heard.

II Esdras 6:32 For thy voice is heard before the most high: for thy righteous, which thou hast had ever since thy youth.

Isaiah 58:8 Then shall thy light break forth as the morning, and thine health shall spring forth speedily: and thy righteousness shall go before thee, the glory of lord shall be thy rereward.

Isaiah 58:9 Then shalt thou call, and lord shall answer.

II Esdras 9:1 Measure thou the time diligently in itself: and when thou seest part of the signs past, which I have told the before,

SKIPPING GRAY MONITORS

II Esdras 9:2 then shalt thou understand, that it is the very same time, wherein the highest will begin to visit the world which he made.

II Esdras 6:25 Whosoever remaineth from all these that I have told thee, shall escape, and see my salvation, and the end of your world.

II Esdras 6:26 And the men that are received, shall see it: and the heart of the inhabitants that be changed, and turned into another meaning.

II Esdras 6:27 For evil shall be put out, and deceit shall be quenched.

II Esdras 6:28 As for faith, it shall flourish, corruption shall be overcome, & the truth which hath been so long without fruit, shall be declared.

II Esdras 6:33 And therefore he sent to shew thee all these things, and to say unto thee, be of good comfort, & fear not.

II Esdras 6:34 And hasten not with the times that are past, to think vain things, that thou mayest not hasten from the latter tunes.

II Esdras 7:27 And whosoever is delivered from the fore said evils, shall see my wonders.

II Esdras 7:30 And the world shall be turned into the old silence.

II Esdras 7:32 And the shall restore those that are asleep.

II Esdras 7:33 And the most high shall appear upon the seat of judgment, and misery shall pass away, and the long suffering shall have an end.

II Esdras 7:34 But judgment only shall remain, truth shall stand, and faith shall wax strong.

II Esdras 7:35 And the work shall follow, and the reward shall be shewed, and the good deeds shall be.

Sirach 50:29 For if he do them, he shall be strong to all things, for the light of lord leadeth him, who giveth wisdom to the: blessed be lord forever. Amen. Amen.

II Esdras 7:64 He is patient, those that have sinned, as his creatures.

II Esdras 7:65 he is bountiful, for he is ready to give where it needeth,

TRUST 1 LORD

II Esdras 7:66 and that is of great mercy, for he multiplieth more and more mercies to them that are present, & also to them which are to come.

II Esdras 7:69 And being judge, he should forgive them that are cured with his word, and put out the multitude of contentions.

II Esdras 9:7 And every one that shall be saved, and shall be able to escape by his works, and by faith, whereby ye have believed.

II Esdras 9:13 And therefore be thou not curious, how the ungodly shall be punished and when: but inquire how the righteous shall be saved, whose the world is.

Isaiah 58:11 And lord shall guide thee continually.

II Esdras 9:19 For then everyone obeyed: but now the manners of them which are created in this world that is made, are corrupted by a perpetual seed, and by a law which is unsearchable rid themselves.

Sirach 3:5 Who so honoureth father, shall have joy of his own children, and when maketh prayer, shall be heard.

Isaiah 58:12 And they that shall be of thee, shall build the old places: thou shalt raise up the foundations of many generations; and thou shalt be called, the repairer of the breach, the restorer of paths to dwell in.

Isaiah 61:4 And they shall build the old wastes, they shall raise up the former desolations, and they shall repair the waste cities, the desolations of many generations.

Isaiah 64:10 Thy holy cities a wilderness.

Isaiah 64:11 Our holy and our beautiful house, where our fathers praised thee.

Isaiah 61:5 Sons of alien.

Isaiah 64:8 Now, lord, thou art our father: we all are the work of thine hand.

Isaiah 64:9 We are all thy people.

Sirach 38:13 There is a time when in their hands there is good success.

Hebrews 4:7 Today, after so long a time: ye will hear his voice, harden not your hearts.

SKIPPING GRAY MONITORS

Hebrews 8:6 But now hath he obtained a more excellent ministry, by how much also he is the mediator of a better covenant.
Hebrews 13:1 Let brotherly love continue.
Hebrews 13:2 Be not forgetful to entertain strangers.
Sirach 8:18 Do no secret thing before a stranger; for thou knowest not what he will bring forth.
Hebrews 13:5 Let your conversation be without covetousness: and be content with such things as ye have.
Jude 1:3 Beloved, when I gave all diligence to write unto you of the common salvation: it was needful for me to write to you, and exhort you that ye should earnestly contend for the faith which was once delivered to the saints.
Wisdom of Solomon 7:10 For the light that cometh from never goeth out.
Wisdom of Solomon 7:17 To know how the world was made,
Wisdom of Solomon 7:20 the reasonings of men.
III John 1:2 Beloved, I wish above all things that thou mayest prosper and be in health, even as thy soul prospereth.
III John 1:3 For I rejoice greatly,
III John 1:4 I have no greater joy, than to hear that my children walk in truth.
III John 1:5 Beloved, thou doest faithfully whatsoever thou doest to the brethren, and to strangers.
III John 1:11 Beloved, follow not that which is evil, but that which is good.
II Esdras 8:2 I will tell thee, the earth, it giveth much mold whereof, even so is the course of this present world.
Revelation 7:3 Hurt not the earth, neither the sea, nor the trees.
Sirach 38:4 Lord hath created medicines out of the earth; and he that is wise will not abhor them.
Sirach 38:7 With such doeth he heal men, and taketh away their pains.

TRUST 1 LORD

Isaiah 29:17 The fruitful field shall be esteemed as a forest.

Wisdom of Solomon 13:11 Now a carpenter that felleth timber, after he hath fallen down a tree,

Acts of the Apostles 5:16 folks, vexed with unclean spirits.

Romans 5:21 As sin hath reigned, even so, grace reign through, right to lord.

Romans 6:4 Therefore walk in the newness of life.

Sirach 14:17 All flesh wareth old as a garment:

Wisdom of Solomon 2:3 being extinguished, our body shall be turned into ashes.

Wisdom of Solomon 2:5 After our end there is returning: so, man cometh again.

Baruch 1:19 This present day, we have been disobedient to lord, we have been negligent in not hearing his voice.

Baruch 1:20 Wherefore the evils cleaved unto us, and curse, it is this day.

Baruch 2:9 Wherefore lord watched over us for evil.

Baruch 3:14 Where is the light of the eyes and peace?

Baruch 3:20 Young men have seen light: but the way of knowledge have they not known.

Baruch 3:21 Nor understood the paths thereof, nor laid hold of it.

Baruch 3:31 No man knoweth her way, nor thinketh of her path.

Baruch 3:32 But he that knoweth things, knoweth her, and hath found her out with his understanding.

Baruch 4:4 Happy are we: for things that are pleasing of lord, are made known to us.

II Maccabees 1:3 And give you all a heart to serve him, with good courage and a willing mind.

Isaiah 42:21 Lord, he will magnify the law, and make it honorable.

Baruch 5:9 For lord shall lead with joy, in the light of his glory, with the mercy and rightness that cometh from him.

SKIPPING GRAY MONITORS

Sirach 43:32 There are yet hid greater things than these be, for we have seen but a few of his works.

Clearings

If you feel negative energy from anyone, quietly, place your left hand high in front of you and swipe down to the ground, slowly, try to feel the lighting of the arm. You will feel a pull down, and when done you will feel a release of the hand. This will clear any soul attachment from a person.

If you kill anything, place both hands above the monster and swipe down to the ground and hold there until you feel your hand being released. This will allow the soul to pass on and not be consumed to all that partake.

If you are eating meat or any food or drink, especially if it is prepared by another soul, place your left hand above the items and swipe down and touch the table or your chair, until you feel the release of lord.

If you feel anger for any reason, you may have a soul attached, place both hands above yourself and swipe all the way to the ground and hold there until you feel the release of lord.

These clearings will work if you believe. Say to yourself, "lord, please clear energy of my soul, this meal, this monster, etc."

Going forward lord will guide you individually on clearing yourself, because it will change with each soul now.

Understand you naturally have free will, daydreaming about the past or future is you not lord, don't meander here long.

After reading this book, lord has assured the author that he will clear your soul of soul attachments, as learning this is a new thing. Start paying attention to little signs in your energy that make you feel bad, learn to clear them right away to keep yourself clear of soul attachments.

Trust lord in all that you do. He will constantly tell you to trust lord as you work with him.

SKIPPING GRAY MONITORS

Your beginning...

www.ingramcontent.com/pod-product-compliance
Lightning Source LLC
Chambersburg PA
CBHW022017160426
43197CB00007B/467